Not Forsaken

This is a True Story and

I'm Still Living It

Not Forsaken
This is a True Story and I'm Still Living It

MARLENE YARGER

StoryTerrace

1

BRAZILIAN CHILDHOOD

"Before I formed you in the womb, I knew you. I set you apart and appointed you to be a prophet to the nations." Jeremiah 1:5 NIV

I'm from Brazil, growing up in a small town of Boa Esperanca, where everyone is friendly and greets you on the street. In English, the town name means good hope. My family is all farmers. There are many farms around the area, which grow mostly coffee, but also tomatoes, cassava, sugarcane, and beans. Outside of town is a large lake. We liked to go there, to enjoy the day and celebrate festivals. I was born on Christmas Day, 1967. We are a family of six girls. I am the fifth, and there is one sister younger than me. Many people in Boa Esperanca practice Catholicism, but in my family, we were not religious. We lived in a small little house, with no power and no lights. It had two bedrooms. I always slept in my mom's bedroom. To get water for cooking and drinking, we had to go to the creek. At night, our only light was a lamp with kerosene.

My daddy worked for a dairy farmer that made cheese. My mother was a chef at a restaurant. My three older sisters all worked in the city for rich people, and looked like my daddy, who had a darker complexion. I was different than all of them—my skin was lighter. I remember my daddy drinking every day. He was a good man, but he fought with my mom. He would accuse my mom of cheating, which she always said wasn't true.

I was scared when he came home, always being drunk on the street. Always fighting, he would start arguing badly. I ran to the neighbor's house every day. As a child, I was very sick with asthma. My asthma attacked the worst when my daddy was coming to the house. I could hear the noise of the cups, and the yelling. One day my asthma was so bad that my mom had to rush me to the hospital. Without a car, we had to walk many miles to get there. She was holding me, carrying me to the hospital. It was so bad, I couldn't breathe. Hooked up to an IV, I stayed in the hospital for fifteen days. When I was finally released, the doctor said I couldn't drink water, but I could drink other fluids. My mom gave me fluids with salt in it. I was so thirsty, that I snuck out to the creek and drank some water. I passed out. My sister said I was going to die.

I didn't die, but never felt included or welcome in my family. When my older sister was eighteen, she married a man. They had a big wedding, where they killed a pig and had all the food. For a time they lived in our house; he was mean. He had a huge temperament problem, always being mean to me and my younger sister. He was a carpenter, building bird houses. He asked us to hold the wood for him. If it was off, he would hammer our fingers. We were terrified of him. We were terrified of Daddy first, then him. To this day I can't stand onions. After helping him with the wood, we came to dinner. I picked out the onions from the beans on my plate. He got so mad at me for picking out the onions he grabbed another onion and rubbed it all over my face and mouth to teach me a lesson. He threw the plate at my sister's head. He was very angry.

The only place I felt safe was with my mom. I would go to school, then go with my mom to the restaurant. I felt safe with her. I don't know if it was because I was sick, but I was her favorite. While she was working in the big kitchen, I'd wait for her. I stayed at the restaurant until she was done. I learned a lot from her. All I know about cooking, I learned from her. To this day, I still enjoy cooking for my family.

By the time I was eight, my older sisters lived in the big city, working as maids for rich people and doctors. They cooked and cleaned for them, living in their houses. With money, they could dress nice, getting fancy clothes. It was not the same when they came to the village. They were about sixteen or seventeen years old. Because they had money and looked nice, everyone in the village was excited to see them. My sisters didn't know what to do with me and my younger sister when tragedy struck our family.

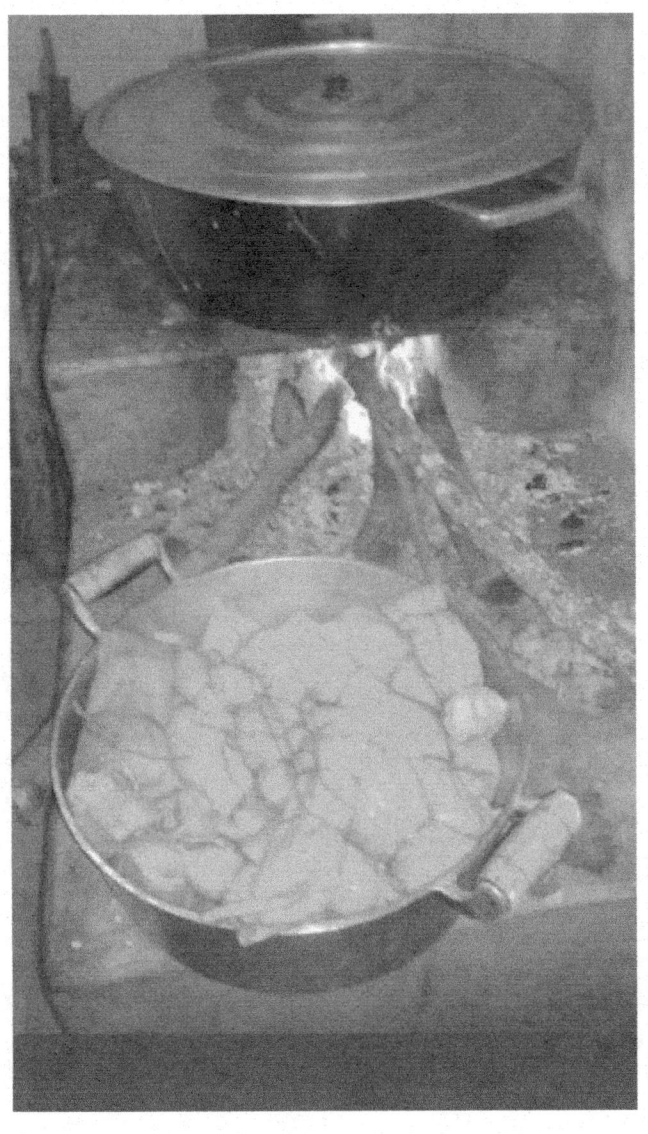

2

LOSS

"The Lord is close to the broken hearted and saves those who are crushed in spirit." Psalm 34:18 NIV

When I was eight, my mom got sick. She was throwing up and weak. She asked me to go to the grocery store and get some tea. When I saw her, she was so sick. She was in bed and not doing well. When she went to the hospital, my oldest sister was already married and had her own place.

When my mom got sick, it was just me and my younger sister at home. I was taking care of the house, at that time kids were left to raise themselves. I would go to school, and come home, cooking for me and my sister. The stove was made of dirt. Each time I cooked, I would make the fire in the pit. Today we are so blessed, with stoves to cook on. Then, we were poor and didn't have much. Every day, I made lunch for my daddy, walking to his work at the dairy farm. It was the same distance away as the hospital, where I had stayed with my asthma. When I arrived, he would give me some milk to drink, and I would head back to school, walking back ten miles.

My dad was continuing to drink, and often came home drunk. For a short time, my mom came home but then got sick again. She kept going back to the hospital. My older sister stopped working, so she could stay with us.

It was sad when someone dies in Brazil, because the body is brought to the house. I remember that day. It was a black ambulance, and the siren was on. It was midnight. My mom had died, and they put her body in the living room, in a casket that was wrapped with purple cloth. It is not like in the United States, with a hard casket. I was crying, and I didn't understand that she was gone.

My sisters came to the house. They wouldn't let me go, and they wouldn't let me say goodbye to her. In Brazil, relatives carry the casket through the streets to the cemetery, and they would not let me go. They were afraid I'd have an asthma attack. The last time I saw her, it was right before they wanted to close the casket in the house. My daddy and my uncle carried the casket to the cemetery, which was close to where my dad worked. I wanted to go, but they wouldn't let me. My mom was everything I had. It hurts me still, that I couldn't say goodbye to her. I will never forget the last time I saw her, laying in the purple casket. She was gone forever. The way she took care of me, she was so proud of me. The images never go away. After my mama died, I never had another asthma attack. Since she was not there to take care of me, I guess God knew I needed to be healed.

My daddy got worse, always drinking, more than ever. My life fell apart, and it was more pain. After she died, he wanted to stay at the bars all night. It was a village where people knew everyone. He was drinking more and more. I'd pick him up at the bars, ten or eleven at night. My sisters went back to work. It was a battle. They needed to know what to do with me. Before my grandfather had died, he had spent the fortune. We didn't have anything.

My sister took me to my aunt's house. My aunt is the younger sister of my mom, and she had one daughter. Holding my hand while we stood at the door, my sister asked if my aunt could take care of me. My aunt looked at me and said, "NO! I don't want another woman to be pregnant."

I didn't understand what she was telling me. I was eight. My cousin was the same age. My older sister took my younger sister. I was still living in our house where my daddy was drinking. At age nine, I went to live with my neighbor, who had two daughters and worked on a plantation. This started a succession of living in different places. Not belonging, and not welcomed, I often felt like I was tossed around like a piece of trash.

3

TOSSED AROUND LIKE TRASH

"Do not be far from me, for trouble is near, and there is no one to help." Psalm 22:11 NIV

While living with my neighbor and her daughters, we worked on the farm and plantations. I was ten years old. Sitting in an open-back truck, we would go to the plantations to pick up coffee, Monday through Saturday. Then we went to the sugar plantation. To collect the sugar, you had to burn the sugar cane. It is like charcoal. Then we used a machete to cut it. After bunching it together, you cut off the top and the bottom. My hands, I remember, were blistered. It was a very hard job. You had to go miles and miles, hunched over. It hurt my back. We also planted and harvested potatoes and picked beans.

For a time, after living with my neighbor, I went back home. My daddy was living in a house, but not the same one where my mother had died. He was still drinking and couldn't care for me. My sister was dating a guy and had a son with him. His brother, who in today's term would be a sex offender, would come to the house when my daddy was out drinking. It was not safe, it had no lock. Running and hiding, I was very scared of him. He would try to touch me, trying many times to hurt me. I lived in fear of his molestations. I had to pick up my daddy at the bar, because he was very drunk. This other guy, who also was drunk, pushed me down. My daddy started fighting with him.

When I was 12, my daddy gave me away to a family who needed someone to cook and clean and take care of her daughter. They had relatives in my hometown. I went to Sao Paulo, to live with a rich lady who had one daughter. She lived in a beautiful house. I thought I'd be loved and accepted but was used instead. I was her slave. Though her husband was wealthy and rich, she'd never buy anything. She was tight with money. Besides me, she was also taking care of a boy. She would make us pick up vegetables from the ground, instead of buying them fresh at the market. She had small houses on the property, which she would rent out to people. Though she was married, she was having an affair with an older gentleman. We would meet him up the hill, having coffee and pastries at a panderia. Then we would go to the property and build more houses. After carrying water from the creek, I had to mix the cement. It weighed about 25 pounds. It was hard work carrying the bricks, and I was so tired. I still missed my mom. At night, the lady would put me in school. She treated her daughter well, but she was not taking care of me. The daughter had dolls and nice clothes. She was given gifts. When we visited the mother-in-law's house, I stayed in the corner with nothing. I had only a corn cob doll to play with. The lady I worked for smoked in the bathroom and had a liquor cabinet. She taught me to smoke. When she was gone, I opened the liquor cabinet, drinking a lot of alcohol. I was passed out on the floor when she came home. She was so angry, she sent me home.

Unable to take care of me, my daddy sent me to a new family, who needed someone to watch their daughter. The dad was a doctor, an acupuncturist. I was to take care of the baby girl. When we would visit his mother, she would teach me how to clean the toilets. She lived in a big house, with a lot of people working for her. I remember I had to scrub the toilet, using my hands. After staying with them awhile, I ran away back to my hometown.

By the time I was thirteen and fourteen, I didn't have a home, or place to live. I had no roots, or place to stay; no bed or closet. I never had a place where they would love me as their daughter. Trying to cope, I started drinking, living at one place, and then the next. When you don't have anything, you don't know where you are going or what will happen. At another place where I worked, I had to wash the diapers by hand. The lady would throw the dirty diapers with the poop still on it into a big container, never rinsing it out. I had to reach my hand in there to get out the diapers to wash them. It was so gross, I wanted to throw up. Everywhere I went, I was used, treated like trash, tossed from one place to the next. I wanted a family to love me, to accept me, to welcome me. Instead, I was treated like an outcast.

4

OUTCAST

"Out of the depths I cried to you." Psalm 130:1 NIV

When my mom was alive, she had a lot of sisters. I had a lot of cousins. My mom loved me so much. On Sundays, we'd all get together, celebrating birthdays and holidays, and having fun. I felt included and wanted, a part of the family.

After she died, I was no longer invited. I felt I was the ugly dog of the family. Not having a place to stay, I slept at my friends' houses. Coming from nowhere, I was a nobody. No one cared about me. I felt my sisters hated me. There was no love, and love is everything. Though my daddy loved me, he was drowning in alcohol. He just didn't care. My sisters wanted to live their own life. Missing the family life, I started hanging out with people with bad reputations, partying the night away.

Staying at my friend's house, I could eat and have a place to sleep. She did not have a good reputation. She invited me to go to the big city, where we stayed with her friend. We always were partying, going to night clubs, where everyone was dancing. When some girls were taking clothes off, I felt uncomfortable. When they would go out partying, I stayed at the apartment. For three weeks we were there. When we went home to Boa Esperanca, I saw her mom whispering in the corner to my friend. Her mom said my dad had passed away while we were gone, and they already had buried him. I didn't get to see him.

It hurt so badly that I would never see him again. I was fourteen years old at the time. Even if he was an alcoholic, and I had to get him from the bars, and he didn't care, he was still my daddy. Even though I wasn't a little girl anymore, it hurt that he was dead. The last time I saw him was when he was at the bar, fighting a guy who had pushed me. I realized my family didn't like me, even though I didn't do anything to them. I was not important to them. They didn't call me or wait for me to bury him. Going to the lake, I cried my heart out. "God, why does this have to happen to me?"

When my dad passed away, it was tough. No one was there for me. I lived with my sister for a while, and they were living on a farm. Her husband was abusive, beating up her son from a previous relationship and tying him up. He'd put him on his knee for hours. Seeing all that as a teenager, I didn't know what to do. My sister, who was scared, didn't say anything. I eventually went to live with friends. I had to fight every day to live and figure out how to make it. I always worked at one house or another, or I worked in the fields. At night, I was drinking and smoking and having fun, living in the moment with my friends.

Sometimes the partying got me in trouble. When I was 18, I wanted to be with my friends at Carnival, a big celebration held in Brazil that occurs right before Lent. Most people in Brazil are Catholic. People dance and have parades with elaborate costumes, partying for four days right before Lent. It is a wild party, like New Orleans but ten times bigger. Thousands of people march in the parade from different age groups. When they are done partying, they move into a time of penitence and fasting. On Ash Wednesday, they get ashes put on their heads, and they fast for forty days, eating no meat and no sugar, and drinking no coffee until Easter comes.

On Carnival Day me and my friends asked someone to take us to the lake to celebrate, near our hometown of Esperanca. This guy that I didn't know agreed to take us. I was sitting in the back of his car. He had a wet cloth that he put over my mouth. After smelling it, I passed out. Upon waking up, I realized he was driving on a dirt road, far away from town. My friends were no longer in the vehicle. Telling me to be quiet, the guy pushed me. He said he had been stalking me for a while. I didn't know what he was going to do to me. I could see the lights of the city far away. When he stopped the car, I jumped from the window. I started running as fast as I could. He was screaming that he would get me. Terrified, I hid in the woods in the dark, not knowing where I was. I was scared and stayed there all night, not moving. In the morning, I walked back to the city. If I hadn't run, he probably would have raped and killed me. I never told anyone. I wished I could have told someone and said something about what happened. But I don't think anyone would have cared.

When I was twenty, I got pregnant. The dad, who was with a lot of girls, didn't want anything to do with me. He said he was not the father. But I knew he was. In Brazil if you are a single mother, you are judged. It is shameful. Everyone said to abort her. I didn't listen to them. Happy to be pregnant, I had something to live for. Since I didn't have a house, I was sleeping at friends' houses. I celebrated my 21st birthday on Christmas by myself. No family members invited me to eat with them. I was seven months pregnant.

In February, I remember celebrating Carnival. I was walking in the parade and started having labor pains. My friends took me to the hospital. All alone, I had no one to support me. I had to have a C-Section. I remember the long needle they poked in my spine. I delivered a beautiful baby girl, Dayane, in February 1989. She was beautiful with dark hair. As I was holding her, love welled up. But I wondered, "What am I going to do for work? How will I take care of this baby?" I didn't have any clothes or baby things, and I didn't have a place to stay.

My friends and my sister all wanted me to give the baby away for adoption. I said, "I just can't give her away." I held her tight, afraid someone would try to take her. Normally, women stay three days in the hospital, then go home. With nowhere to go, I stayed in the hospital three weeks. If you are a single mother in Brazil, only your name is put on the birth certificate. The father's name is not put on there.

My ex-boyfriend said, "You can give her to me. Me and my mother will take care of her, and you can see her occasionally." He wanted to put his name and his mother's name as the mother on the birth certificate, taking my name off. I couldn't do that, giving up my rights as a mother.

My sister, the one whose husband had abused her son, said I could stay with them. I was afraid for my daughter. It was only a week. Feeling uncomfortable there, I was scared for my daughter. Her husband was angry, wanting me to leave. One day a little bag of clothes was put outside. He had tied up my clothes, tossing them out on the street. Poop was inside the bag too. Grabbing my daughter, we fled. I was scared, not knowing what would happen to us.

Riding a bus for eight hours, I went to live with my former neighbor, whom I had lived with after my mom died. The lady had moved. It was the same situation, with an alcoholic. She suggested going to her sister, who lived on the beach. At the beach house, the people had a small house, where workers stayed and took care of the place. I worked for the sister, cleaning the beach house, and watching my daughter, who was two years old. It was complicated and hard to do both.

I got a different job and found a place to stay. While I was working, the people I lived with watched my daughter. From the money I was making, I had to give it to them for diapers and milk and food. I couldn't touch anything in the house. My daughter had beautiful hair. It seemed like they were jealous of her hair. One day after coming home, I saw the people had cut her beautiful hair, like a boy. My daughter was crying, and the milk she had was bad. Instead of using the money I gave them for her, the people were using it and giving the best to their own daughters. We had been sleeping on a twin mattress. When my daughter peed on the mattress, the people took it away. We slept on the floor. They were very mean and started beating my daughter. Being dependent on them, I was very scared and afraid to leave. It was the only place we had. Working every day, I would come home to wash clothes and helped in the house. When we were watching TV, my daughter was picking up trash and missed some. They spanked her so hard.

I said, "Please don't do that!"

When I stood up for my daughter, they kicked me out. They grabbed my long hair and pulled it. They tossed my clothes out on the street. Getting my daughter and my clothes, I didn't know where to go. That area where we lived was dangerous. There were guns, and gangs, and sex offenders. I was so scared, walking on the road with my daughter. I didn't know where to go. Trudging ten miles in the dark, I went to the house of a friend, whom I used to date. My friend wanted me to live with his sister, who was married and worked at a house where they offered sex. I couldn't do that. I was trying to find a way where I could have a normal life. I wanted to have a bed and a place to stay where they wouldn't use me. I wanted someone to love me as I was.

5

ROMANCED

"I have found the one whom my soul loves." Song of Solomon 3:4 NIV

I found an older lady who had rooms to rent—a place where four girls lived. Though I didn't have money, she agreed to take me and helped me find a job. While I worked, she watched my daughter. At night I was a bartender and I cleaned houses during the day. Things were getting better, and I was feeling good. I could buy things for my daughter. I felt stable, like things were looking up for us. Life was better, but I still wanted my own home. I was looking for someone to marry, to have a home, a husband, and a better life for my daughter. My daughter's father and I started seeing each other again, but it did not last long.

He said, "I am sorry that I was not there for you."

While I was working, I always rode the bus. The bus stopped at a checkpoint. The police were looking for someone who had committed a crime, who had a gun. A guy on the bus moved toward me, putting a gun in my purse. He warned me not to say anything. Shining their lights through the bus, the policemen looked at everyone and their belongings, even in my purse. For some reason, they didn't see the gun. It was God's hand that covered the gun. I could have been put in jail.

I was doing a lot with one of the girls who lived in the house. We would go to her family's home on the beach and hang out together. Her family did not know she was doing drugs. One day, in a location away from where we lived, that girl was found dead from an overdose. Knowing her and where she lived, I had to tell her mom she had died. That was hard.

With the two other girls living in the place, we still spent time together. We decided to travel to from Sao Paulo to Rio De Janeiro, which was eight hours on the bus. The lady who owned the house where we lived said she would take care of my daughter. I was twenty-four years old.

While visiting Rio, we went to see Christ the Redeemer Cross, which is a large statue with Christ with His arms extended. It was beautiful, rising above Rio on a hill. It stands nearly 124 feet high. Visitors go there to take pictures. All around the area are restaurants and gift shops. We met three men there. One of them was French, who left his home and went to the United States when he was sixteen. He had dual citizenship in both countries. His Portuguese was bad. The men invited us to dinner at a fancy restaurant. It was the three of them, and us three girls. I remember the forks and spoons, so many forks, and the fancy tablecloths. Growing up poor, I had never eaten at such a rich place. After dinner, we partied at a night club, dancing through the night.

Connecting with the man from France, I stayed the night with him. He seemed interested in me. He asked me to fly back with him to Sao Paulo where I was living. It was my first time on an airplane. When I got on the plane, I was thinking that things might improve for me and my daughter. My friends took the bus back.

While we were staying at a 5-Star hotel in Sao Paulo, he was treating me very well. He was giving me roses and gifts and buying me expensive clothes. He took me to fancy restaurants. I thought, "Is this what it's like to be loved?" I loved the attention, even felt giddy. I had never been treated like that. It felt heavenly.

He kept telling me he loved me. Though I speak Portuguese and don't speak English, and he spoke mostly English and French, we communicated. He was twelve years older than I was. He went back to the United States, and called me every day. I was still in Brazil. We were falling in love. I was walking on the clouds.

When he said he had never been married, I believed him. I felt like my life and my daughter's life was about to get better. He said he had money, and that he worked. His family was from France, his dad a doctor. He had come to the United States when he was sixteen, later going to college and becoming an American citizen. He enjoyed traveling all over the world. He kept telling me he was never married, and I was his first girlfriend, that the women in Brazil are better than women in the United States. Women in the United States don't want babies, he said, only money. I was proud to have a boyfriend who was American. He was good at manipulating me, and making me be in love with him. We kept it up for several years.

Saying he loved me and wanted to marry me, he proposed in 1993. He gave me a ring, a diamond ring. In Brazil when you get married, it is usually just a wedding band. He promised to adopt my daughter. He kept giving the impression that he was a good guy. He bought me a wedding dress from an expensive store in Los Angeles. When I received the dress in the mail in Brazil, it was weird. In Brazil, the woman usually buys the wedding dress.

We were married in my hometown in Boa Esperanca. He went to the newspaper to have it published. Many relatives came to celebrate, thinking I was doing well, congratulating me. At the time, my relationship with my aunts and my sisters was better. They were thinking I had money, that I was somebody. We had a reception at a restaurant afterwards, on the lake. He was giving everyone the impression that he was a good guy.

My husband said he'd pay the bill, but never did. When he wrote a check at the restaurant, it was from the United States. The restaurant owner said he couldn't accept the check because the bank wouldn't take it. My husband never paid for the wedding. I was so disappointed. My cousin was saying everyone was talking about it, that the wedding was not paid. I felt shame. I got it in my head that something was not right. When it came time to fill out the marriage certificate, he was not present. He was traveling out of the country. In Brazil if you get married, you must show a birth certificate. In a phone call, my husband said his birth certificate was burned in a fire. You must also not be married to someone else. He was always telling me, he had never been married before. He had a lawyer in Brazil fill out paperwork, which I had to sign. My husband was not there, which became a pattern throughout our marriage. I was so giddy in love, walking on clouds, I could not see the signs that he was lying to me.

6

BETRAYED

"Whoever desires to love life and see good days, let him keep his tongue from evil, and his lips from speaking deceit." 1 Peter 3:10 KJV

When he returned to Brazil, we lived in an apartment in Sao Paulo, but quickly fell behind on payments. He said he was working, but I didn't know what he did for a job. I believed he was working for a company in the United States. We had moved to a smaller apartment. We always were fighting about money. I got a job, working to help people get insurance.

My husband was traveling a lot, leaving me alone in Brazil. Months went by, the rent was not being paid. I tried talking to him by phone. Making excuses, he said that his brother was robbed and shot in the head. He was staying in France to be with his brother. I was crying for him, saying "I am so sorry." A week later he called, saying his brother had died. I was traumatized for him. In France, his family was waiting for him to celebrate his brother's life. It is usually a long celebration, about a week. More time went by. He was not paying the rent. When we talked on the phone, he said his mother was so sad about his brother's death, that she had a heart attack, and she died too. Then, his father got sick and died. After all that loss and tragedy, I thought, "Oh my gosh, I feel sad for you, that all these relatives have passed away." My heart was full for him. I believed what he was telling me. I was blind. The communication was difficult. He got a friend to help me move to a cheaper flat.

Three months went by. I said, "You have got to come back. We are married."

After three months, he returned to Brazil, moving us into a bigger apartment. Opening the mail one day, I saw a picture of him with another woman. It was a lady with dark hair and skin standing with my husband. She had the last name of my husband, Goubert. When I asked about it, my husband said it was his cousin's wife. He was trying to cover it up. In my heart, I was feeling something was not right. I had a bad feeling. He was getting upset, verbally abusing me. He was not violent with me. Only one time, he hit my head on the mirror.

Another letter arrived in the mail to us in Brazil. It was the writing of a girl. I saw the letter, but I couldn't understand it. Inside the envelope was a picture with two girls, also having his last name. It was not the same picture that I had seen before with the black lady. Having a bad feeling, I thought he was hiding something. We were always fighting about money. He was getting mad and upset. We had to move to a smaller house, and our money situation was not good. He didn't get a job, and never worked. My cousin said I should have the letter, which was written in Spanish, translated. It appeared the letter came from a girl who was his daughter, who was saying she hated him and would never forgive him for what he did to her mom. My husband had told me many times that he had never been married before.

I had to confront him. Why was he lying to me? He was covering up, not telling me the truth.

Though I did not understand what he was doing, we still had a relationship. I got pregnant and delivered a boy, William, in 1996. It was at the same hospital that I delivered my daughter all alone, where I ended up staying three weeks because I had no one to help me. This time, I wasn't alone. Many relatives came, my aunts and my sisters came and celebrated, even my husband seemed to be excited to have a boy. It was good when my son was born.

Money was tight—we had no money to buy groceries. I was thinking, "How in the world could he go from being rich, to having nothing?" I started working again, selling insurance. I bought insurance for my children. My sister came to stay with us, to take care of my daughter and my son, who was six months old. While I was working, my son had started walking. My husband was outside, not paying attention. My son, who was in a walker, went out the door and fell. I came home from work to see him crying. He hit his head, his eye was big and all swollen, requiring him to go to the hospital.

While riding the bus to go see him at the hospital, I had to grab the bar above me to hold on. My purse was full, I had just gotten paid. Someone stole all my money. I was crushed. At home, I was always arguing with my husband that I was the only one working. After getting evicted, we kept moving. My husband said that it was time to move away from Brazil. I found out that his parents and brother were still alive in France, and they never passed away, like he had said.

7

FLIGHT TO FRANCE AND BACK TO BRAZIL

" I f I rise on the wings of dawn, if I settle on the far side of the sea, even there your hand will guide me." Psalm 139: 9 NIV

For a time in 1997, we moved to France, where my husband's family lived. My daughter was nine and William was one year old. We stayed with his brother the first night. His brother, who also had married a Brazilian, was talking to my husband in French. His brother was angry. After picking us up, his daddy drove us nine hours to his parents' home in Ales, which is near Montpellier. It was a beautiful little city and very cold. It was the first time I saw snow—it was so pretty. When I met his mother, I knew my husband had lied to me about their deaths. She was a nice lady, who liked to dance and drink Tequila. They lived in a beautiful, big house, as his father was a doctor. Because I didn't speak the language, I couldn't understand what they were saying. While my husband talked to his mom and daddy, I would talk to my daughter. I felt lonely there. My husband was always fighting with his father. We lived at his parents' house for six months. I couldn't understand the language, but I could tell my husband didn't have a good relationship with his dad. They were always angry at each other.

After moving back to Brazil, I got pregnant again. My husband was accusing me of cheating, just like my daddy did with my mom. It wasn't true. This time when I delivered another boy, Kenny, I was alone again. It was July 1998. My husband was traveling and was not present for his birth. I had to get my ex-boyfriend to bring me home. Everything for my husband was for my older son. My older son, he was the most beautiful boy as a baby. All the nurses wanted to hold him and keep him. My husband was excited when William came home. That was not the case with Kenny. When my husband came home two weeks after Kenny was born, he had no affection for Kenny. It was difficult. He did not have any feeling for this unplanned baby. Later that year, my husband announced that we must move to the United States. I was feeling scared and excited. I was not sure if I could trust him since he lied about his relationships and where he was traveling, and his parents' deaths. I was thinking, "Where is he going to get the money?" Even with everything my husband had done, I had to go with him. In Brazil, once you marry someone, it is for life. My children got their passports. All my children became United States citizens by him. For people coming from Brazil, going to the United States is a dream, and a ticket to a better life.

8

STRUGGLING IN THE UNITED STATES

"So do not fear, for I am with you, do not be dismayed, for I am your God. I will strengthen you and help you, I will uphold you with my righteous right hand." Isaiah 41:10 NIV

When we came to the United States in January, 1999, I was excited to live here. I expected to have a better life and better opportunities. My daughter was nine, turning ten shortly after we came. William was two years old, and Kenny was six months old. We moved to Greenville, South Carolina. Seeing the lawns with lots of grass and yards and big homes was amazing. At first, we went to the house of one of my husband's friends, whose name was Brenda. We met her husband. She arranged an apartment for us. I was getting excited to live in an apartment. It was all new. My husband planned to work for her, doing parties. She was interested in doing business with him, but she did not really know who he was.

But the reality of living in the United States was not what I was expecting. When we moved here, it was rough. It was a tough time to adapt here, especially with the food. In Brazil, we eat rice and beans, and vegetables, and meat. I was not used to the fast-food or culture. Not speaking English, I couldn't understand what people were saying. My husband would not let us speak Portuguese in the house. To help us, some of the church ladies would come to the house, teaching my daughter and me basic words in English, like plate and fork.

A few months after we moved to the United States, my husband left me, going back to Brazil, and staying for a month. It was a scary time, being in the United States alone with my kids, not speaking the language. We were running out of food. My husband's friend Brenda, the one that helped us move in, came to check on us, but we couldn't understand each other. She brought us some food. I also attempted to go to the grocery store. Wandering around the store, what seemed like forever, I was looking for rice and vegetables. This lady who spoke Spanish asked me if I needed help. I understood a little Spanish, trying to explain what I needed. She was able to help. I was so grateful.

When my husband returned from Brazil, it was stressful. My husband would take the kids to school, and to their doctors' appointments, in the guise of being a good dad. Later, I would find out, he was having documents signed that would take the kids away from me, and talking about me behind my back, that I was a bad mother. When we went to church, I felt uncomfortable, not understanding English.

He never hit me, but he did verbally abuse me. We were fighting a lot, usually about money. I never knew what he was doing for work. We were having problems. I had to be careful of him, and I was scared. When he came back, he left receipts on the table. It was all in Portuguese from gift shops and purse shops, extravagant items. It was all gifts, like he used to buy for me.

Why is he buying all this stuff? I thought. I was 100 percent sure he was cheating on me, because of all the receipts. That he was with another woman and buying her stuff.

In 2001, we moved into our first home in the United States, living there for two years. He did not put my name on the title. My husband got me a job at Cookies by Design, which was close to our apartment. We decorated cookies. I became one of the best decorators. Not speaking much with the workers, and not knowing much English, I came in and did my work. I was there working on Sept 11, 2001, when everyone stopped and watched the TV as the towers fell. I didn't understand what was happening. When I came home, my husband told me that the towers were bombed. It was very sad.

After working at Cookies by Design, I got another job, decorating cakes at a grocery store called Publix. My English wasn't very good, and it was very hard to learn. Because I was a good worker, my manager asked me if I would be willing to close the store at night.

"No! I couldn't be myself, I don't speak English," I said.

But she put me there anyway. I thanked her for giving me the challenge. When I started closing the store, I was so nervous. When you don't speak English, you speak it badly sometimes. I was scared to speak it. I figured it out and taught myself English. I just needed to open my mouth and speak, eventually getting better.

I kept working, standing on my feet for hours at a time, decorating cakes. I was good at my job. But it was taking a toll on my body. My legs were hurting, and my knees were tight and swollen. My ankles looked like elephant feet. It was scary.

After taking a blood test from me, my doctor said, "I have never seen a person as young as you have rheumatoid arthritis. You have bones like an eighty-year-old woman."

She referred me to a specialist, who was from India. We had a hard time communicating. He told me I would need to replace my knee, and I couldn't stand on my feet while I was working.

Not heeding his advice, I continued working anyway at Publix. While working there, I built up my credit and I had my own car, a Ford Explorer. It was in my name. I had credit cards and made payments on time. I had good credit. I had a checking account, and took care of myself.

My husband was traveling all the time. When he came back, he left papers on the table. It was a court paper. I saw his name, and the lady's name. She carried his name, Goubert. It was the same lady that I had seen in the picture, the one I had seen in Brazil after we had first gotten married. She had dark skin and dark hair. Laying on the table in the United States many years later, that paper I saw was a divorce paper. Shocked and dismayed, I realized he had never divorced his wife. That is why he couldn't be at court in Brazil or sign the marriage certificate when he married me. When he married me, he was still married. I also found out he had been married before her. I was devastated.

9

DEVASTATED

"Do not turn me over to the desire of my foes, for false witnesses rise up against me, spouting malicious accusations." Psalm 27:12 NIV

Finding out he had been married, not just once by twice, was devastating. When we were dating, he had told me he never had been married before, that I was his first wife. I felt betrayed by him. I was thinking, "Why did he have to lie?"

When you marry in Brazil, you must have a birth certificate. You cannot marry again if you are still married. At the time when we got married, he said he didn't have a birth certificate because it had been burned in a fire. When I found out the truth, I became his enemy, he felt threatened by me. He started telling people at church that I was an alcoholic and on drugs, that I was a bad mom. People were looking at me. The pastor was judging me. Feeling uncomfortable, I did not know what he was saying about me. I felt shunned, pushed away.

He kept traveling and doing his thing. Our marriage was

awful. I found another letter. It was a picture of a woman from Bolivia, the letter was written in Spanish. In Brazil, we speak Portuguese. He had promised to bring her to the United States. He said he was a widow, that his wife had passed away. Not speaking the language, I didn't know what to do. Brenda, the lady who helped us move in, also was mad at him, not understanding what he was doing.

When my husband came home, he was getting calls from the other woman. He started being mean to my daughter. Things were bad between us, we were always fighting. When we'd go to church, he was telling the people that I was a bad mama, and that I was doing drugs and alcohol.

In 2002, I asked my husband if I could go to Brazil to see my family. I took my son Kenny, who looks like his daddy with his light skin. I have dark-colored skin. When we were trying to leave Brazil, we had problems at the airport. My husband, who had gotten the passports for my children, did not put my name on Kenny's passport. To get back to the United States, I had to use my Brazilian passport.

Things were getting worse between me and my husband. We were always fighting, mostly about money. When I was at work, he was treating my daughter badly. I never knew if he was doing something bad to her. I said we should separate and get divorced. Always putting me down, he snapped back, saying that he had power, that I was nothing and couldn't take care of my kids. If we got divorced, my daughter would end up as a prostitute and my sons would be nothing, just like I was when I was a kid. He said my sons would land in jail. I was stuck with no way out, scared he would do something to hurt me and my children. I started calling him nasty, for the women he had been with.

In 2003, my husband arranged for me to go to Brazil, to talk to someone about his company business. Promoting it as a great opportunity for me, he said he would take care of the kids. At the airport as he was dropping me off, I had a bad feeling. He gave me money to rent a car in Brazil. My daughter and William were in school. He was holding my youngest son Kenny, glaring at me. He said, "Just remember the one who is nasty."

Carrying my Green Card, which permitted me to be in the United States, I flew to Brazil, unsettled and unsure what would happen. To get to the scheduled business meeting, I drove with my cousin for eight hours. My husband had flown from the United States, in the guise of attending the same meeting in Brazil. It was with a sugar company and some leaders were there in the room. While we were sitting in this large room in a hotel, the phone rang. The businessman handed it to me. It was a lady, asking for my husband.

Stunned, I said, "I am his wife!"

"He told me you were dead," she said.

I was so upset. My husband told everyone to leave the room. It was just me and him. I exploded at him about the phone call.

"How can you bring me here and have your girlfriend call?"

Crying and crushed in my heart, I went to the bathroom to wipe my face. I had left my purse, with my Green Card on the counter in the other room. He had told his girlfriend to come and be with me in the bathroom, while he was still in the big room. He had calculated everything, planning what he would do. With eyes red and swollen from weeping, I asked my cousin to go back. I needed to get back to my kids.

As we were driving the eight hours, I told her that when I got back to the United States, I was getting a divorce. After arriving at my aunt's house, I felt something was telling me to check my wallet. I looked in my purse. My Green Card was not there! It was gone. I asked my cousin. She said she had not taken it. I knew my husband had planned everything. He had taken my Green Card when I was in the bathroom crying. When I called him, he denied he had the card, saying I was stupid for losing it.

"I am going to the American Counsel to tell them I lost my Green Card," I said.

"If you go to the American Embassy, you will be put in jail," my husband said. I didn't understand what he was saying. I hadn't done anything wrong. I was scared. Knowing he had done something terrible, I was terrified.

Without the Green Card, I couldn't get home to my three kids in the United States. He planned it, to keep me there in Brazil. He was trying to get rid of me, so he could bring the other lady to his house in America. When I would call to talk to my kids in the United States, he made excuses, saying they were out or couldn't talk to me. I could never talk to them, my sons. He was taking that from me.

At the time, we were living in our second house in the United States. Days stretched into a month, I was still trapped in Brazil. I didn't know what to do. On my son Kenny's birthday on July 6, I was still in Brazil. He was turning five years old.

I called my husband, "Please let me talk to my son and say Happy Birthday to him."

Refusing, my husband said Kenny was with friends and couldn't talk to me. I couldn't understand, I didn't do anything. I was a good wife, cooking for him and cleaning his clothes. He wanted to get away from me. I was depressed that I would never see my kids again. In America, he was trying to show my kids that I had abandoned them. Trying to delete the memory of me, he was saying that I wouldn't come back. My daughter knew it wasn't true.

I was staying at my aunt's house in Brazil, feeling so low in my life. I was sleeping with my kids' picture every night, thinking, "This is all I have." In my heart, I was losing hope to see them again. I was dealing with someone with so much power, my husband could do anything to hurt me. He had a lawyer in Brazil come to me with papers, declaring a divorce. I never knew anything about it. My husband had not said anything to me about getting a divorce. Signing the papers would mean I would never see my kids again. I didn't sign the papers.

"After I go back to the United States and see my kids, I will sign," I told the lawyer.

With so much anxiety, I had to take medicine to calm me down. Several times I went to a medium, who used Tarot cards to help make sense of everything that was happening to me.

Twice when calling the house, I got through to my daughter. When my husband was outside, my daughter answered the phone.

"Where are you?" she cried.

"He has my Green Card, I cannot come home," I replied. My heart was breaking. When he saw her on the phone, he was furious and was yelling at her. I found out later he pushed my daughter down the stairs. Another time when he was sleeping, she called me in the middle of the night, telling me the names of ladies she saw on his computer.

While I was living at my aunt's house, the phone rang. We were sitting outside. The guy on the other end asked to speak with me. My heart pumped. I didn't know him or why he was calling.

"Don't ask who I am," he said, "But I know someone planted drugs in your aunt's house. It is enough to put you in jail for a long time. I am calling you, you must go look. You must find the drugs. You don't deserve to be treated that way."

Hanging up the phone, I was stunned. I felt paralyzed. My cousin asked, "What is wrong?"

"We need to check the house. Someone called, saying drugs are in the house."

Trembling at this news, we searched all over her small house but couldn't find the drugs. We searched again and again, in every corner and every room, but found nothing. The man called again, asking if we found them. No, I said.

"Look again!" he pleaded urgently. "You have got to find the drugs. They are in her home. If you don't, police will come to arrest you and put you in jail." Looking again, all over, we finally found the bags stuck in the rafters built between sections of the house. It was in a room where my uncle keeps his fishing gear and tools. There were three big packets of drugs, wrapped in duct tape. My heart was pounding so fast. All I could think is, if the police show up, I would be arrested. I was terrified of losing my life, of never seeing my kids again. We knew a policeman who was also a friend, and my aunt called him at work. After he finished working, he agreed to come to the house to examine the drug packets.

"Oh my God," he said. He had the drugs tested. It was expensive cocaine paste, worth about $10,000.

Furious, I called my husband. "How can you do this to me?"

"Do what?"

"Planting all these drugs. You are trying to get rid of me."

"You are crazy," he said, denying it all.

If we had been caught with those drugs, we would have

been locked up forever. The policeman had the bags of drugs disposed out in the woods, sparing our family. It was God's hand, protecting me. The man who called about the drugs the first time called again. He was relieved that we had found the drug packets.

At one point, the phone rang again. The man said I needed to run, because guys were coming to my aunt's house and planned to shoot everyone. A hit man had been hired to kill me. I ran to a friend's house to get away. My aunt and her family left and were also able to get away. Every time I confronted my husband, he denied it.

Seven months dragged on, and I was desperate to see my kids. All this time, the lawyer in Brazil kept calling me. I was ready to make a deal. If my husband would take me back to the United States, I would cook, clean, and take care of the kids. His other girlfriend could come to the house. My husband called me at my aunt's house.

"If you sign the papers, you won't work. You will stay in the house and not have any friends," my husband said. I agreed to sign the papers, which meant I couldn't go anywhere, couldn't answer the phone, couldn't work once back in the United States. I was doing anything to look at my boys and hug them, to be with my daughter again.

My husband came to Brazil to get me. I was so afraid. I knew I had married an unstable person. It was like the movie *Sleeping with Enemies*. I said I didn't have my Green Card.

"We'll figure it out," he said over the phone. "Go grab your stuff. We are going to a hotel." I had to ride eight hours on a bus to get there. You don't know what's going to happen if you will live or if you will get killed. I had to do it for my kids. The whole trip on the bus, I was thinking in my mind, "He is going to kill me. He will hide my body, and I will never see my kids again."

We stayed at the same hotel in Sao Paulo where he romanced me so many years before, after we had met at the Christ Redeemer Cross in Rio. He came to me in the hotel, after he had been with his girlfriend. This time when he had sex with me, I felt so dirty. I felt violated, after everything he had done to me. I didn't want to be with him. He was not the man I married. In his face, I didn't see any remorse. Eyes wide open and terrified, I couldn't sleep. He got up, saying he would be back. I waited hours and hours for him to return. When he did return, he said we couldn't leave that day, but would move to another hotel close to the airport. Not knowing what would happen next, I had to do what he said.

When the taxi driver arrived the next morning, he talked with my husband, who was sitting in the front seat, like they knew each other. Briefly, my husband stepped out of the taxi to take care of some business. The driver turned to me in the back seat, handing me his business card and said, "If you ever need help, call me. I can help you. You do not deserve to be treated this way."

I held his business card in my hands, astonished. I had heard those words before. It was the same words that the guy said when he called my aunt's house about the drugs. I knew it was the same man. God had sent him to help me.

That night in the hotel, my husband left me alone. Terrified, I stayed up all night, looking at the door. In my mind, I am thinking he will kick in the door and kill me. Every sound, any noise I heard, I thought it would be somebody sent to kill me. I did not sleep all night.

When he came to get me the next day, we drove to the airport to check in. He pulled out my Green Card from his wallet. I knew he had lied but couldn't say one word. I wanted to see my kids. I went home to the United States, and cried when I was able to hold my kids. To hold them in my arms was beautiful.

Will Goubert graduated magna cum laude from North Greenville University on April 28, 2018. He received his Bachelor of Arts in Spanish and Christian Studies. Will is serving as Youth Pastor at Double Springs Baptist Church in Taylors, and will also be teaching Spanish at an area high school beginning this fall. Will is the son-in-law of Chad and Stephanie Sheriff.

10

REBUILDING

"And the God of all grace, who called you to His eternal glory in Christ, after you have suffered a little while, will Himself make you strong, firm and steadfast." 1 Peter 5:10 NIV

Seeing my boys and holding them in my arms back in the United States was the best thing. I had been gone for seven months. When I left for Brazil, my daughter was in middle school. I had lost almost a year. When I returned, she was in high school. We went to see her there. She had completely changed, she was different and beautiful. I was thrilled to be with my children, even with the restrictions. I signed the papers. At the house, I couldn't go anywhere or answer the phone or get a job.

I asked my daughter, "Dayane, where are my clothes?"

My closet was empty. It had no clothes or shoes, except for an expensive coat that my husband had given to me. He had planned to give the coat to the new girlfriend. All my stuff was gone. My daughter showed me where they were.

Jamming the clothes in a bag, my husband had put them downstairs, away in a back room. After taking my Green Card, he never expected me to come back. The clothes were wet and moldy. My car, which I worked for by decorating cakes at Publix, had been taken away. My credit, which had been good when I lived in the United States and before I was trapped in Brazil, now was bad. To take care of the bad credit, my husband said I should declare bankruptcy. I didn't understand what he was doing. I was traumatized. He constantly would talk on the phone to the other woman. But while I was there in the house, he expected to have sex with me. It made me sick. This man tried to kill me! I did it because I was scared.

One time I answered the phone while he was outside mowing the lawn. The lady was from the bank, asking for William. She said his credit card was in collections, and he owed money. I was stunned. Checking into his social security card, I saw my son had $45,000 in debt! When I confronted my husband, he denied it. When I again asked for divorce, he sneered at me and called me stupid.

I was crying constantly. My husband was taking the kids to church and out to eat, putting on a face that things were alright, while I stayed home. He was backstabbing me, talking about me as a bad woman. One Sunday while I was alone sitting on the porch, I talked to God. I thanked him for bringing me back to my children. But I didn't want to live with my husband. I was constantly living in fear.

Looking down the road, I saw cars were speeding toward me. I wanted to go down there, so a car would kill me. I felt ending my life would fix my problems. I felt a hand on my shoulder, "It is not your time."

Not feeling well and coming back into the house, I took some Nyquil, and laid down to rest. I was powerless, I didn't have anything to prove what he had done. Everyone trusted my husband, to them he was good. But I knew he was not.

Exhausted, I did not hear my husband come home with the kids. My husband said, "I must go to Brazil." While he was gone, something spoke to me, and pushed me to go downstairs. I felt in my heart, "You will find what you need."

Looking behind the computer, I saw a packet. When I opened it, I gasped, "Oh my God!" It was pictures of him and his girlfriend at a restaurant, her with teddy bears and flowers. Him, smiling and drinking champaign. Her naked. Other pictures showed him and her with flowers, partying the night away. I also saw emails of them communicating back and forth, and other correspondence between him and contacts in Brazil. One email confirmed what I thought: It showed $10,000 that was spent to buy drugs in Brazil. It was at the same time when I was trapped in Brazil, and we found the drugs planted at my aunts' house. He had planted the cocaine there, expecting me to get arrested and thrown in jail.

I was shaking, my heart pounded. It was what I needed. God gave it to me. I was able to talk to a friend, who helped me to get an attorney. I showed him the pictures. He agreed to take my case, even though I didn't have much money. A different lawyer agreed to handle William's case, which had the credit card with his name and $45,000 dollars charged on it, that were not his purchases. While the lawyer was figuring out what to do, I took my kids to eat at a Chinese restaurant. I saw the pastor and his wife from the church who had judged me.

I asked them, "Can you come to my house? I have something to show you." They came, reluctantly.

Grabbing all the pictures, I said, "I am sorry for what you will see. This is the man, who came to the church, with a Bible in his hand. He talked about his wife. He comes home and treats me like a slave." That pastor had trusted my husband but had spoken badly of me. When he saw the pictures, he was shocked. His eyes got huge. He apologized.

"I am so sorry," he said. Very embarrassed, he asked me to come back to the church. I didn't want to go.

The lawyers told us to leave our house, and not tell my husband I had left. While my husband was partying in Brazil, I gathered all my stuff and the kids' bed and clothes and moved to a small one-bedroom apartment in the city. The apartment was not in a good area, but it was what I could afford. My husband kept calling from Brazil, wondering why I was not at the house. I was scared to have him come home. He made me think I was nothing, that I couldn't take care of my kids. It was emotional and verbal abuse. He made me think that if I left him, my kids would end up just like I was, alone and destitute. He made me feel like I was his property, like a slave. The situation was delicate. I prayed, "God, just hold him there."

He stayed in Brazil for two months. When he returned to the United States, he knew something was not right. He called the house, but I didn't answer. He called my cell phone. I was at work.

"What did you do? You will pay for this." He was screaming at me. My heart was beating so fast. Gathering strength from inside, I took a deep breath.

"You don't scare me anymore." I hung up the phone.

The lawyers said, "We have to serve him the divorce papers."

Driving by our house, I saw that my husband had a Ford truck in the driveway. It looked like he was getting ready to move and sell everything in the house. I quickly called the lawyer. We planned what we would do. I was hiding, my husband could not see me. When I saw him leaving, I contacted the authorities.

I remember as my husband was driving away from the house, I was on the phone with the person who would serve him the divorce papers. I was on the road in front of my husband. He could not see the other vehicle approaching. I was close to the stoplight, and it was turning yellow. My husband had to stop. The law enforcement officer got out, handing him the divorce papers. "You have been served."

After contacting his lawyer, my husband moved. He sold the house. My lawyer arranged the first meeting at the courthouse. I was nervous to see my husband and face him. He didn't show up. His lawyer said my husband was in Brazil. I had to go to court four times. He never showed up, always giving excuses. The judge, who spoke Portuguese, told my husband's lawyer, "I am sick of him not coming." To me, the judge said I was free to go. God gave me a gift, that I didn't have to see my husband.

The judge granted the divorce and required my ex-husband to pay child support of $1,000 a month, plus $200 in alimony. My ex-husband did not pay the money. I had never told my kids how bad he was. It was very hard on them, they were asking where their daddy was.

The judge also ordered that the safe box, which my ex-husband had at the bank, be opened. In the box were lots of papers, including my children's passports and many documents signed by doctors, saying he was a good dad and I was a bad mother. There were some papers from the box that I did not look at until 2021. My ex-husband had been contacting the Embassy in Brazil in 2003 when I was trapped there, telling them I was a criminal and should be arrested if I tried to leave. He intended all along to get rid of me, but God had other plans. With all that my husband did, with all that darkness, I could have died. It was only by God's grace I am alive.

After the divorce, I was free to rebuild and start a new life.

I continued to live in the small apartment with my kids for a year. Accusing and judging me, my husband had always stated that I couldn't make it, that I couldn't take care of my kids. Proving him wrong, I worked hard and became successful. I applied and starting working selling cars at a dealership, not knowing English well. The dealership was owned by a man named Todd, who lived in Tennessee, and was managed by his brother. His brother knew my situation, that I needed to work after my divorce. Out of great kindness, he allowed me to drive one of the cars from the dealership. While I was working there, I did very well. I was very blessed. I became the saleswoman of the month, seven out of the eight months I was there. It seemed impossible with not knowing English, but I did it. But with God all things are possible. In January 2004, I met Todd, who had come from Memphis to check out the business. He was driving a Corvette.

"How can I help you?" I asked.

"You can park my car," he said, smiling.

We began talking and an affection between us started to grow. It is very hard to talk about this. Before you know God, you do things in the world, not knowing it hurts God and is sinning against Him. Todd went back to Memphis, and we started seeing each other and having an affair, as he went back and forth between his home and his business in South Carolina. At the time, he was married and had a daughter in high school. He said his marriage was not going well, and he and his wife were sleeping in separate rooms.

He wanted a divorce from his wife but wanted to wait until after his daughter finished high school and was in college until he did anything.

After working at Todd's dealership for eight months, I went to work at another car dealership, providing for my kids. Todd and I continued dating for one year. In 2005, we suddenly stopped talking to each other. Todd said I had to give the car back, which I had used from his dealership. We had no contact and didn't hear from each other. There was no communication between us. I had several other relationships, and even got engaged to a man who was a nurse, but he was not the right one and it didn't work out. I would date other men, but they were not good for me, always pulling me away from God.

My boys would come to the new dealership, being there and doing schoolwork from 3:00 p.m. to as late as 11:00 p.m. They were so good, sitting there for so long. I was good at selling cars, often winning saleswoman of the month, many months in a row. I was able to rebuild my credit and eventually buy a house. I wasn't going to church, but my boys were going with their friends. When their dad called, they talked to him in the beginning. But eventually William didn't want to talk to him anymore.

Time passed. Fourteen months went by. My ex-husband was behind on all his child support payments. Altogether, it was about $14,000 that he owed me. He called, saying he was coming from Brazil and wanted to see the kids. I could not trust him. I was afraid he would take the kids. I called the lawyer, wondering what to do. The lawyer said, "We can get him for not paying child support." In South Carolina, if you don't pay child support, you can be put in jail.

My ex-husband and I planned to meet at Applebee's. I was there with my kids, waiting. When I saw him, it had been over a year, and it was weird. I wanted him to see my kids, but I didn't know he would be arrested that day. When he arrived, the lawyer and a police officer were ready for him. My ex-husband was arrested outside of Applebee's and put in jail. But he got out after one night! Somehow, he was able to obtain $14,000 to pay back all the child support and got out of jail. I don't know where he got all the money. It was such a blessing to have all that money all at once. The money helped me take care of my kids. We were able to move from the small apartment to a house. It was the only money I ever saw from him. As my children were growing up, I constantly felt God's hand of protection over our family, keeping us safe.

My sons never gave me a problem when they were growing up. My sons, they never went out and partied. When they did go out, it was with friends from church. I see God's hand in that. I had so much responsibility to raise them. They were kind and respectful to each other and to other people. When I would bring them to work at the car dealership where I worked for 17 years, my coworkers got to know them. If you sell cars, you clock in, and then clock out hours later. It is all commission-based. We were always there for hours. I asked my boys to be good, and they always listened. Never running around, they sat quietly and did their homework. Even when they needed to go to the bathroom, they would ask me. At the end of the day when I would say it was time to go, they would be sleeping. I took them to bed at home. Then at 6:00 a.m. the next morning, it would start all over again. I sometimes asked, "How is this possible?" I couldn't do it alone. People wondered why I would bring my children to work with me. I had to, to make it. It was God who helped me. Sometimes I cried and I was exhausted.

When I got divorced, I was leaving a bad marriage. I could have given my kids away. I could have given up, but I didn't. My boys are very special to me. As a single parent, I worked hard for them, trying to give them more than what I had growing up. As a child, I didn't have a birthday party or Christmas gifts. I had only one pair of shoes. After my parents died, I was not invited to family celebrations. I wanted their lives to be different from mine. Raising them by myself after the divorce, I was able to provide for them and give them gifts. If I could buy it, I did. Once a year, we went to the beach.

When we got divorced, my daughter was a teenager, and my son William was eight years old. He was very smart. He always liked to read, bringing a book everywhere, even when we went to the beach. He didn't need help in school. Getting awards in school and for projects he created, he also won the Spelling Bee in middle school. He met with the Governor of our state when he was ten years old. He had always told me his goal was to graduate and become a doctor. He wanted to buy me a big house, so I didn't need to work again. When he was fifteen, he said he changed his mind, wanting to go to a Christian school and be a missionary instead, even if it didn't make much money. I broke down and cried, that he was wanting to follow God. That same year when he was fifteen, we experienced a heart-stopping event. I had left work early that day and came home because I was sick with a high fever. After going upstairs, I had fallen asleep, sweating so badly and feeling very thirsty. Kenny also was upstairs. My daughter was out of the house by then. When I came down to get a drink, William was at the table, his face towards the kitchen, looking at his laptop. I was talking to him, and he was not answering. His head was down.

"Don't play with me," I scolded. I noticed there were letters on the screen and his hands were shaking. I didn't know what was happening. As I was hugging him, his mouth was twisting. I laid him on the ground. I started screaming. Kenny came down. I called 911. It seemed no one was answering. I was crying, pleading for help. I threw the phone down on the ground. I was so scared he was gone, I started pushing all the buttons on the house alarm. The fire department, police, and ambulance all showed up to my house, all the emergency people came to help. They said he was having a seizure. On the way to the hospital, he had another seizure. His heartbeat and oxygen were low. He spent two weeks in the hospital. The doctors didn't know why he was having seizures. They gave him medicine, which seemed to help. After that, praise God, he never had another seizure. I believe God sent me home that day, when I was sick, so I could be there for him.

Graduating with honors from high school, William attended a Christian college in South Carolina on a full-ride scholarship. He studied Christian missions and Spanish. While in college he went on a mission trip to South America. He said, "We are rich in the United States. We are serving meals here to people who live off the dumps, making one dollar a day." Now he is a teacher and has a job as a pastor at a church.

With Kenny, as the youngest, he was like my baby. He was six when I got divorced. He was completely different than William. I had to be on top of him in school. He ended up being the tallest in the family. Because he was a big boy, I wanted him to play football. He didn't like the tight pants. William would help him with schoolwork, when I would bring them to work with me at the car dealership, after they were done at school. As a teenager, Kenny struggled because his best friend committed suicide. It affected his schoolwork and life. I had to take him to a counselor. Eventually, he followed his brother to college, and now serves as a counselor to teenagers. Awesome as a team leader, he is leading many kids to Jesus.

My daughter didn't end up going to college. When she was seventeen, she got pregnant. She is now married and has three children. We had been through so much when she was growing up. I am so glad that I made the decision to keep her and raise her. We have a good relationship. Living close by, she visits me often.

In 2016, I studied to become a citizen of the United States. I listened to a CD, going over 100 questions on American History that they could ask on the test. The test would have ten questions, and I could only miss four to pass. I studied so hard and didn't miss any! I was so proud to become an American citizen. All those words my husband had said about me were not true. I was smart and capable, and with hard work, I could take care of my kids.

My ex-husband left the country, never paying child support again. He called me, saying he was in Africa. He was asking me to forgive the large amount he owed me, so he could bring his children from a new relationship to the United States. He knew if he came back to South Carolina, he would be immediately put in jail for not paying child support. After much prayer, I decided to forgive the amount, even though he had hurt me so much. Later I would find out from his friend that my ex-husband had hurt other people, too. In and out of relationships with women from many different countries, he had fathered fourteen children who lived in several continents. He has since passed away, dying a broken man.

Looking back, I don't regret my decision to forgive that debt. Though he had hurt me, he was still the father of my two boys and had adopted my daughter. Through him, I was able to come to the United States and meet God and know His love.

11

EPIPHANY AND TRIP TO ISRAEL

"I will never leave you or forsake you." Deuteronomy 31:8 NIV

My daughter kept asking me to go to church. Leery after being hurt at the other church where people had judged me, I didn't want to go. At the time, I was living with a man and partying hard on the weekends. He was only with me because I was working and had a house. People had warned me about him, saying he was a "player" who would be with women and take advantage of them. I couldn't see it. Lonely after my divorce, I needed someone to be with me. He had a lot of small personal loans, for which he kept getting collection calls. I helped to pay all those bills off. I also helped to pay off a car title of his ex-wife. She was about to have her car repossessed. Knowing that she was a nice lady who was working hard, I felt bad for her and agreed to pay $5,000 to get the title so she wouldn't lose her car. While we were together, I met my boyfriend's mother, who was in a nursing home. She was a sweet lady, and she loved me. I got to know her when we visited. When she died, my boyfriend did not have the money for a funeral. Using money from my 401K, I helped to pay for her funeral. I took a big hit, withdrawing money early. After the insurance money from her came into the funeral home, the funeral home paid me back some of the money. The whole time I was with that boyfriend, I was feeling something wasn't right.

My daughter kept inviting me to church. Eventually I went, just to get her to stop asking me. I called my boyfriend, asking him to come too. As soon as I walked into the church, it felt different than the other church. I felt peace, and I felt welcomed. I could feel God's presence in the place. When the pastor was preaching, it seemed he was speaking directly to me. Every word hit me. As soon as he asked people to come forward and receive Christ, I was out of my seat. I accepted the Lord that day. Joy filled my soul. I felt the Lord's presence wrapping me like a warm blanket.

Going to church, I felt accepted and loved, and started to serve, taking care of the babies in the nursery. But I was still partying on the weekend and living with this boyfriend, who was taking me away from God. He was draining me, dragging me away. We were fighting a lot. On every Friday and Saturday night, we'd go to the bar and drink and dance, then go to church on Sundays. I felt embarrassed and ashamed of myself. The pastor was preaching about how people lived one foot in the world, and one foot in the church. I was feeling miserable. We were fighting a lot. I was feeling like I wasn't doing something right.

When I was working and he was at home doing nothing, I felt he was doing me wrong. I went into the bathroom at work and cried. My heart was aching.

"God, why is my heart so tight?" I thought I was going crazy. Throughout the day, the feeling of tightness kept getting worse. "God, if this feeling is from you, show me what to do! If it is just my mind, then just take it out."

After work that day, I went straight to my daughter's house, who lived five minutes from work. She had invited me for spaghetti dinner. I called my boyfriend and let him know. He came to her house about nine o'clock to join us.

When he came in, I looked at him and his face. I knew something wasn't right. After we went home, we were getting ready for bed—we always went to bed at about ten o'clock. After brushing my teeth, I was in bed, and he was in the bathroom. Something was telling me to go into the bathroom where he was, and I would find what I was looking for. He was texting someone.

"What are you doing? Who are you texting?" I asked him.

"I am texting my daughter."

"Let me see."

"You are crazy," he said, pushing the phone in his pocket.

At that moment, I knew he was texting another woman. He denied it. When I confronted him and told him he would have to leave, he got violent. He grabbed a cup of water that was on the counter and threw it against the wall. I felt pain. I felt betrayed, after everything I had done for him. I didn't know what to do. While he was with me, he was paying the cable bill. When I got the cable bill later, it was $600. I was shocked. It turns out, he had a porn addiction and was watching porn at 5:00 a.m. when I was sleeping. Sometimes, he would be watching on Sunday mornings before church. I felt ashamed. After he left, I cried a lot. I dragged myself to work, working twelve hours, then came home and drank through the night.

Most nights I wasn't sleeping well. I had a dream, I saw Jesus in the clouds. He was extending His arms to me, welcoming me. I was feeling so much pain, from paying all that boyfriend's bills, and the deceit. I was hurting. Jesus was saying "Come to Me." I felt His presence and His peace surrounding me.

I told God, "I don't want to be in a relationship with a man who drags me away from You. I want a man who worships You and reads his Bible. I want a man who loves You and loves me for who I am. Together, I want to be able to discover more about who You are. If there is not a man like that, then I don't want to be with anymore. With Your strength, I will make it by myself."

Though I was hurting, I loved reading the Bible and spending time with God. God was everything to me. I didn't want to be in a relationship with anyone, I just wanted Jesus. My daughter was married, my sons were in college.

Even though I was lonely, I had to keep it going. After working, I would come home, drinking so I could go to sleep at night. I didn't go out on Saturday nights anymore.

In February 2018, I had a chance to go to Israel with my church. It was an amazing experience. Twenty-one people from the church went with me, including our pastor, and a man named Chuck, who had helped start the church, and his wife Kathy. We visited many areas. It was wonderful to experience where Jesus walked with disciples, where He preached to the people. We stayed there for ten days, visiting a different place each day.

At the Dead Sea, people said you can't sink. I didn't believe them. We all went. The moment you go to the deep water, your feet go up. I didn't sink! It was so amazing.

We visited Bethlehem, where the city has two separate places where locals say Jesus was born. The Catholics built a big church that you can enter. The side for Christians was small. You go into a cave. The feeling was amazing. You can feel God's presence. When we got out of the church, you could see the moon behind the cross. It was delightful!

We saw the sun rise at the Sea of Galilee. It was dark when we came. We had a guitar, we were worshipping God. We saw birds flying above the water, and boats coming in. As the sun was coming up, it was gorgeous. It was a beautiful moment. I had a lot of beautiful moments in Israel. Going to Israel changed me. It was a great experience. When you go there, the Bible comes alive. I was walking where Jesus walked and standing in places where Jesus stood with his disciple, like at Peter's house.

We went to the Garden of Gethsemane where Jesus wept and prayed as he was preparing to be crucified on a cross, so many years ago. While others in the group were among the trees and praying, I was sitting there, talking to Jesus. I was weeping, feeling the brokenness in my life. Both my parents had died. I had been abandoned and forsaken much of my life, betrayed by my husband, and nearly murdered. I was ashamed of my past. The pain and loneliness overwhelmed me. Chuck and Kathy, who were part of the group from our church, heard me crying. Hugging me, they prayed with me. It was a beautiful moment. In that moment, I felt peace. I knew Jesus was there with me, holding and reassuring me.

One day when we went to dinner, I began to share about my experiences and the pain I experienced. My church friends were crying as I shared. We talked for about two hours.

"You have an incredible testimony. You have to share it with others," they said. Kathy, who had prayed for me in the Garden of Gethsemane, suggested that I should write a book. I felt for the first time that someone cared about me.

Another highlight of the trip was getting baptized in the Jordan River. When we walked there, the place was packed with a lot of people. Standing in line, I was shivering in the wind. It was so cold going in, it was freezing in February. I put my feet in the water, and it was freezing. I didn't know if I could go through with it. Reluctantly, I went in. I was dunked, cold water splashing over me, and I came back up. After being baptized, I expected I would feel chilled, being soaking wet and in the wind. Instead, I felt warmth in my feet going through my legs and up into my body and head. I felt heat, up to my head. I asked my pastor what that was. He said it was the Holy Spirit on me, warming me up. It was amazing, getting baptized in the Jordan River.

Everyone says going to Israel will change your life, and you will never be the same. I took more than 2,500 pictures. At every place we went, I collected a rock. I have two pounds of rocks from Israel. I often was the last person to get to the bus. When things open again after the pandemic settles down, I would love to go back there. The people that went, we became close and still are good friends. Chuck said I was like his daughter. All my life, I was looking to be accepted, and with this group, I found people who would love me and cherish me.

Returning to South Carolina, I got close to God. Feeling good, I was feeling joy in my heart. I have the joy of Jesus in my heart. Nothing can replace that. I love to read my Bible, discovering who He is. I began serving more in the church, helping in the nursery with the kids, helping on Wednesday nights. I was still working hard but not needing to drink alcohol as much.

One day while I was out running errands, I stopped at a red light. I had a vision. My whole life flashed before my eyes. God showed me my life: my daddy drinking, when I was sick with asthma, when I lost my mom and my daddy, when I met and married my husband in Brazil, betrayal, and moving to the United States.

He said, "I was always with you, I never have forsaken you."

As the light turned green, I was crying so hard, saying "I'm so sorry, that I always said, 'Why, God? Why is this happening to me?" I did have a lot of pain growing up, but He took me through all of it. I began to thank Him I was alive, that I had two beautiful children with my former husband, that my children love God, that my daughter married and has children. That my sons went to college and are serving him. One is a pastor, and the other works as a youth counselor. I always have prayed that my sons would be honorable men, and not like their father. God answered those prayers. I was never alone. I thanked God for bringing me to the United States so I could meet Him and understand His love.

12

WEDDING BELLS AND BAREFOOT ON THE BEACH

"I have loved you with an everlasting love." Jeremiah 31:3 NIV

The God who created me, loves me. I pray every day that I can be a light. People say that I am shining. Only God can take you through all of that, all the danger I went through. Life can take joy from you. Everything that I experienced, I didn't understand. I have scars. I felt broken by my experiences. But God carried me. Like a shepherd looking for a lost sheep, he left the 99 sheep to carry me. When I opened my heart and let Jesus and God in, He began to heal my heart and all the broken pieces. Throughout my life, He was holding me. I know God is close to the broken hearted. Through all the pain, He never let me go. I have been able to forgive my ex-husband, my auntie who did not want me after my parents died, and my sisters who didn't care for me. When I was living one foot in the world and one foot in church and living with my boyfriend and partying all the time, I felt Satan was taking me away. But God wouldn't let him. God was carrying me. After reading the Bible from beginning to end, I understand who Jesus is. He is the Son of God, who died for me. He forgives me. I am close to God. I know that I am here today because I have something to do, especially helping people who are hurting. I can tell them how good God is, and you can have a relationship with Him. Now that I know Him, I wake up happy, and go to bed happy. The joy comes from the Lord. I want to show the picture of joy you can have when you have Jesus in your heart. I love God so much. I'm alive, I'm here. I am so blessed.

Loving Jesus, I was finding I didn't need a relationship to fill my needs. But I was still longing to have someone by my side, to have a friend I could talk to. "God," I remembered praying, "I don't want to meet anyone. And if I do, I want a man that will talk to me, and pray with me, and take me to church. I want someone who will read the Bible, and worship You, who will love me for who I am."

I had seen on Facebook that Todd had been and engaged and married a second time in 2017. I had put him out of my mind.

One day after work in 2019, I saw I had a missed call from Todd. We hadn't talked for fourteen years. I was very surprised. How did he get my number? I had changed phones several times. I couldn't understand how he found me. I texted him back, saying, "Is this you, Todd?" He said it was him. We started FaceTiming. After he asked me how I was doing, I started talking to him about how close I was to God, that God and reading the Bible were important to me. I told him I had been working hard, which enabled me to buy a house. He was very impressed with all of that.

He shared how he was having problems with his marriage. I told him we could pray for his marriage. I love to talk about God, and the goodness of God. My intention was to have a good conversation about God, leading him to the Lord but not to get involved.

One night after work I was watching TV at my house. Todd called, "Do you want to have coffee?"

"Coffee?" I was surprised. "It is too late, it is nine thirty." I usually went to bed at ten.

"Do you want to have breakfast in the morning then?" He was in town, picking up a car from his brother's dealership where I formerly was employed.

Unsure and anxious, I agreed to meet him. We met at a restaurant, near the car dealership where I was working. It was weird in my heart. I hadn't seen him in fourteen years. My heart was shaking. I was thinking, "God, please, I can't do this again. Why is he back in my life?"

He was married and getting counseling. At first, I was afraid of doing it all again. The first time we dated, he had been married to his first wife, and ended up getting divorced. This is not possible, I thought. I prayed a lot. I could feel the enemy was trying to trap me, to take away all the goodness that God was giving me. At the same time, I was having feelings toward him. I texted him, "I don't want to have anything to do with you, you are still married."

Though we were not dating, we still were talking on the phone. During this time, his wife had moved out, separating from him. Over the phone, we started reading the Bible together in the morning and he'd pray with me at ten o'clock at night. We'd pray, then I would go to sleep. We did that for a year. I was beginning to see that we were doing what I had prayed for in a relationship.

His divorce was finalized Dec. 15, 2020. We started dating. He would come here and stay at a hotel, instead of my house. I didn't want to be tempted and be living in sin, as we had before in the affair. When we were dating before, Todd went to church, but didn't read his Bible. The second time around, we were reading the Bible in our relationship. I told him that God must be first.

In December, he proposed. It was unreal, how this was all happening. It was incredible that though we had a dark past, we were together. We knew it had to be God. We were engaged. He said, "We have to get this right and get married." He said we should get married at our church.

I wondered, "Just in a church?" That was not how people in Brazil got married. They have a wedding and people come to celebrate with you. Fighting Todd on the idea, I just didn't want to do it. My dream had always been to get married in a flowing dress with no shoes on, on a beach with white sand.

The pastor said he had seen it many times, where the couple says their vows in a church, then has a bigger marriage celebration later. Following his suggestion and because we wanted to honor God with our relationship, we had a small, quiet ceremony on Dec. 23, 2020, with just our pastor and his wife, and a few other people in the church.

In the springtime on April 8, 2021, I got my dream. We flew to Destin Florida, where Todd had a condo. The sand on the beach is white as snow. God is so good. On my wedding day, the weather called for thunderstorms all day. It was raining in the morning and predicted to rain in the afternoon.

"God," I prayed, "I am grateful for the rain. I love the rain. But can you please give me one hour of sunshine around five o'clock on my wedding day?" God opened the sky and cleared the clouds away, and the sun was shining. It was a beautiful day. The sun dried the white sand. My younger son Kenny walked with me. My son, who is a pastor, married us. My daughter and my three grandkids were there. Todd's children and some of his grandkids were there. Chuck and Kathy, the friends who shared a trip to Israel and first heard my story, were there. The day was perfect, perfectly fitting the dream that I had. It was simple and gorgeous. Adorned in a flowing white dress, I was barefoot and beaming on the beach, believing that God always has been with me, and that I am loved.

StoryTerrace